LOVE
LESSONS

POEMS 1973-2023

Mary Ellen Capek

Book design by Sara DeHaan

Printed in the United States of America

Publisher's Cataloging-in-Publication data
Names: Capek, Mary Ellen S., author.
Title: Love lessons : poems 1973–2023 / Mary Ellen Capek.
Description: Corrales NM: Arbor Farm Press, 2024.
Identifiers: LCCN: 2024906116 | ISBN: 978-0-9855200-6-9 (paperback) | 978-0-9855200-7-6 (ebook)
Subjects: LCSH American poetry—21st century. | Biographical poetry, American. | BISAC POETRY / Women authors | POETRY / LGBTQ+
Classification: LCC PS3603 .A74 L68 2024 | DDC 811.6—dc23

For Sue . . . and for Mike

CONTENTS

ACKNOWLEDGMENTS

Thanks to Kathleen Hill, who heard or read most of these poems as they were first written. Spanning almost sixty years, our long friendship has meant the world to me. (Kathleen's latest book, *She Read to Us in the Late Afternoons: A Life in Novels,* is a stunning memoir.)

Thanks also to others who've made helpful suggestions and encouraged their publication: Rebecca Aronson, Linda and Gloria Bailey-Davies, Sue Hallgarth, Lynda Miller, Lynn Miller, Susanne Page, Patti Peterson, Jaune Quick-to-See Smith, Hilda Raz, Ruth Rudner, and Stephen Yenser. And a special thanks to Sara DeHaan for her design skills and support getting this book to print.

A shout-out to Hilda Raz (*Letters from a Place I've Never Been*); Lynda Miller (*More Horses Than Cars: A Memoir*), Lynn Miller (*The Lost Archives: Stories*); and Jules Nyquist (*Atomic Paradise*)—all inspiring writers themselves—for the creative work they do bringing community to writers in New Mexico through *ABQ inPrint*, Bosque Press, and Jules Poetry Playhouse.

Jaune Quick-to-See-Smith was the inspiration for "Asylum," sharing knowledge of the Incas' khipus, their "language of animals." The title of the poem "All My Relations," which also comes from Jaune, is a phrase used by Indigenous people to express the interconnectedness of all creation.

"Asylum" and "Pink" were previously published in *ABQ inPrint*, 2019 ("Asylum") and 2023 ("Pink").

"I Dream of Dead People" was previously published in *Persimmon Tree,* Spring 2021.

.

LOVE LESSONS

Dancing Class

We danced in the school basement.
Strauss waltzes mingled with the smells of chocolate milk
and stale peanut butter sandwiches,
bits of Wonder Bread like paste wax smeared across the floor.
We ducked bare bulbs that swung too low,
making awkward shadows on the posts.
Steam in the pipes beat its own dance tunes.
I dreaded Tuesday afternoons.

"Boys, choose partners."

Red-faced and nervous, they eyed us from across the room
then jostled for the few girls wearing bras.
The rest of us lined the wall and waited to be touched.
Or paired by size.

Five-eleven in my socks and flat-chested, I was never chosen.
I danced with our teacher or Bert,
as fat as I was tall, who later did time in Rahway
for running down an old lady
in his '48 Dodge convertible.

Elaine was always picked.

She wore 34B in the sixth grade, was fast, Jewish, and my best friend.

For her, I stepped on cracks and once, on a dare, farted in class.

Her father, a widower, hired housekeepers with carrot hair

who told us dirty stories.

One sang to herself,

"Don't ever let 'em get you in bed until you've been to town."

Elaine once told me, scared, "Boys only fuck you when you bleed."

(Or was it the other way around?)

I ran home from school one day in tears, ashamed, screaming,

"Shit, you shit, you bitch" across the street.

Elaine had led a chorus chant that afternoon,

"Mary Ella has no fella tiny tits and giant feet."

"Boys, take the lead. One and two and dip and...

No she dips, Bert, not you."

The needles of their laughter stuck and warped our moves.

Chosen or not chosen, we measured time by twos.

Dawn

The sun at island's edge casts chains into the night,
rings of light bind shores and lake.

(Old myths tell of men too early come,
caught in light too early seen,
lost in golden, blinding mist.)

A fisherman throws his lines;
the glass shatters, its mirror breaking glistening arcs.
Rings of his cast scatter to shore.
Across the water, a silver fish breaks surface,
metal in air, a moment arched, he flakes water in sparks of light.
A gull, white-winged, swoops through the trees,
circling the waves, hovering, poised.

The fisherman watches, new light shading the morning breaking.

Sensuality

Contrary to all my liberated fantasies,
when making love to you
I long to be swept off my feet
and spun like cotton candy in your mouth,
sweet fluff that melts to crystal,
smearing the shadows of your sly grin.

Instead, stiff with fear,
I'm a cardboard cone stripped of sweets,
a scared kid on the Palisades Tilt-a-Whirl.
Leaving, I tense a smile, hug you,
then trudge off into the cold night,
scraping powdered snow like icing from my windshield
with bare hands.

Shopping for Patterns

Trying to make up my mind between the Charmeuse, Crepe du Chine,
    or natural raw silk
for a Vogue American Design I'd finally settled on
after an hour of thumbing through pattern books,
I couldn't help overhearing the women talking near the polyester blends.

Acquaintances, apparently for years, the one with a pretty, teenaged
    daughter by her side
was blonde and sad, with the middle-class WASP beauty parlor look one
    step up the social ladder from all those Toni home permanents my
    mother'd tried for years on both of us.
(Before she died, my mother found Blanche at the Belmont Beauty
    Shoppe,
who for $20 bucks could give her curls that would outlast any Toni.)

But where was I?
The other woman, owner of the store, had been saying that
so many of her friends were getting a divorce. A widow, she didn't
    understand.
The ME generation and all that.

The mother with the curls began to set her straight: divorce was hard,
but sometimes a woman had no choice.
Her husband, after 23 years of wedded bliss, had just run off with a
    young cutie
who worked in the neighborhood bowling alley, renting shoes.

The shop owner switched her take:
"But of course if it doesn't work, it's harder on the kids to stick it out.
It becomes a lie, I guess."
(Not to mention impossible if your husband spends his days in bowling
    alleys, renting shoes.)
She'd once had a friend who'd been divorced, almost since his son
    was born,
and the son had never known anything different
so assumed all kids spent weekends in different homes.

Both women spoke as though the daughter wasn't there.
I felt sorry: her mother must have suddenly remembered
she was old enough to hear.
She turned and said to take a walk, to wait outside.

The girl, embarrassed but with dignity, refused,
and the mother, grim lines set around her mouth, spoke briefly of her
    own pain
and weakly finished with frustration.
"We'll talk more when Carol's not around," she said,
looking impatiently at Carol, who stared at the floor
but exchanged shy, knowing glances with me over the corduroy.

To Wait

I'm dead-empty but the door's unlatched.
What's fear? An empty house, reflections in the window.

On a dark night, I watch and remember:
"Human beings," I recall, "need…
need five-six hours of sleep a day (night)
to maintain a healthy organism."
Or is it more?

I go eight to ten, sleeping finally at dawn.
I am tired, dead-tired.

Fear spoils my thoughts.
My stomach pit's a knot.
Irony washes out like a tide that ebbs with no high,
edges hot in its wake.

Wind lashed against the glass can't dry a wet face.
The only thing that's left? To wait.

Inside This Cave

Inside this cave, the mind is black and damp,
no light, no shadows.
Walls stream with water. I can go no further.
A rock: I bend to pick it up
but stop before I have it in my hand.
No need. I can't see.
Only dampness and dark.
I think my hair's in curls.

I have stumbled on this place by accident while out walking,
but I have been here before. This dark's familiar.
Dampness shapes my skin. My hands know moist.
Here I am one—my skin's the cave's walls.
In depths, I melt the blackness.

All My Relations
(Blackbird, Spider, Crow)

Blackbird

A blackbird fat with spring seeds, worms, and winter's rest
swoops to the curb puddle,
poises a moment to test water with a curious beak,
then lands,
little caring he has just felled a tree.

With a splash, fluid branches break in endless circles.
Chaplin-like, he leaps through rings
and stretches like a well-fed male,
smug with self-assurance.
He's soon caught in his own motion,
nipping, flapping, flapping faster and faster.
The whole curb corner's filled with flying water.
Broken lines of tree and sky explode.

A dervish clown menaces the calm afternoon reflection in the sun,
until—with a flash and a flick of his wings—
he's gone.

Spider

I awake to the acrid smell of a spider crushed in sleep.
All night long I lay with the corpse.
Her filaments, dashed and broken lines, are tangled on the pillow
where my thumb must have caught her crawl across my bed.

Smeared, she's a pungent slash of orange,
a gay, abandoned pattern on my sheets.
I dreamt witches burned at sunrise seek revenge.

Crow

The Interstate winds like a scar ribbon
through fall woods the color of Indian paintbrush.
I pretend I tread softly on beaded moccasins,
belonging here, akin to the black crow
catching the last rays of sunset and
bowing the top branches of a maple
reddened to the colors of blood and Sassoon pink.

Coming Home

The bus tunnels into the darkening night.
Distant sparks of light
glint off the black walls closing in around us,
protecting stiff winter dusk like the studs of my worn leather belt.

I'm reading Adrienne Rich and getting depressed.
I can't argue with her tormented vision,
bruised violence, bitter nostalgia that tracks her common
    language dreams.
But her wild patience aches.
Where's the peace?

She re-members. I am driven to forget,
to reach my hand through broken frames of glass
as though the last brass ring
were creaking on a rusty arm.
I grab the blur of spinning neon gold
and studs of light explode like the
wedding bands I've buried in my sleep.

A Language of Our Own

for Adrienne Rich

Grabbing words out of thin air
like brass rings on a merry-go-round,
I'm a tin ear.
False notes shatter cheap crystal in the wrong case.

I need tongs and a forge,
hammers to beat dead metal into sparks, old maids, and angels
naming red hot mysteries, furies that endure.

My head's a furnace,
spitting fire and weaving curls of light.
I fume and stitch and dream of Eleanor Roosevelt
carved in profile on Mount Rushmore,
woven through the hot mat on my stove,
cigar clamped boldly in her teeth.

A glass bowl pops in white heat.
I turn in sleep, flesh on a skewer.

Awake, here's a self, parsed in my father's verbs and puns,
a slice, razor-thin and sterile, stuck on a slide.
Each cell contains the universe, my universe a cell.

I spin like a child's kaleidoscope.
Wired phases.

Forget the furnaces and cells, my sweet.
Grow like a turnip, waxed and solid underground,
or fly like mustard seeds each spring
to root and sprout on barren ground,
brash yellow in the sunshine,
dancing on lithe stems in soft, spring twilight.

Be instead a raucous mountain stream,
streaking in the moonlight over rocks,
wearing down the slopes of earth
to shape the thrusts of its own passing.

Share words like spume and mist, water mossed or clear
fanned against rocks,
or catch the tones of a woman, warm and languid,
crooning her child to sleep in the sultry, late summer air,
spinning golden sighs and syllables of plaited silver.

And Why Don't You Write?

for Sarah Hill

> And why don't you write? Write!
> Writing is for you,
> you are for you;
> your body is yours, take it!
> —Hélène Cixous

At thirty-six, I'm a child's kaleidoscope,
filled with shards of multi-colored glass.
The spinning doesn't stop.

I try to memorize one shape,
hold it like a fossil embedded in soft stone.
My foot's on the floor, but the whole room shifts.

Shatter the case:
words fly out like moths that tangle in my hair, my mouth,
worms that burrow in my skin.

I feel them curling in my blood,
more intimate than the curve of my thighs,
the shape of my thumb, the anger of old love.

Wired phrases.
These are words from a dictionary written in small print
that buzz like clumsy mosquitoes in my ears
or pop, ripe elderberries in my blood,
bursting small veins.
Chords of laughter echo
like the Medusa on Hollywood and Vine.

I don't belong here.
These are poems from another climate too hot to handle.

Dying for Art

in (bitter) memory of Anne Sexton

I challenge Anne and her poems to death.
I'm sick of dying.

I watched my mother die.
She lived with the Sign of the Crab.
Ashen and scared, she cried to be free,
dreamed she was buried alive in a gray metal coffin.

She'd tried death too—
pills when she knew she was full of it.
But they brought her back, cheap pimps.

Where was her silver needle?
Those last few weeks of pain she clung to life;
one breast gone, her black necessary trousseau sagged.
Her eyes glazed with pain.

But Anne, that whore, played
Death & Co., a weak imitation,
played a living out of dying and conned herself dead.

Critics mourned—
She had no skin, no edge against the pain.
She suckered death and made it ART.

A poet's skin is raw, Anne.
But you splayed yours
then called them "naked" poems.

My mother's dreams:
all the little children,
are they off to school?
September in May. Shy girls in crisp plaid ribbons.
Slicked-down boys. The desks in rows.
They sent her poems and tulips.

Grandfather's house. The toy castle.
A bell that rang and rang. The house, the castle, and the bell
all buried in dreams. Althea that child.
I held her hand. She cried when she soiled her gown.

But Anne's a cheap strip-tease.
She drops her drawers and shows her ass.

She aches for God and thinks she's Christ,
the most artsy double die-er of them all.

Shove it, Anne. You had a choice.
You sell your poems and throw in funerals free.
Althea died. No poems. No fall. Not free.

I'm not buying.

Friendship

Come with me and
you'll sing like a raucous crow,
hit notes you never knew you had.
Tired?
I'll tuck you into crisp white sheets
that smell like grass in warm spring yards.
I'll draw the shades and
play you an afternoon tune on my harmonica.

Awake?
I'll slip you strawberries
steeped with currants in May wine
then send you home,
packing my songs to go.
You conduct yourself with dignity,
but I expect you'll come another time,
your own maestro,
then pluck more harmony with me.
Chords that fine
need stops to savor time.

Returning

Your Christmas box, returned unclaimed from Kenya,
arrives back home the same day you do,
tan and rumpled like the once-crisp wrappings
now festooned with colored stamps,
marks of agents not accustomed to such self-control.
You'd refused to pay the tax.

Not hearing, I'd assumed the L.L.Bean white polo
intended for your swimmer's chest
got bartered in some thatched back room
and now stretched willingly to fit the broad black shoulders
stroked by languorous hands in equatorial moonlight.

Mimicking prayers,
my fingers twist the beads you brought,
polished nubs of green striated stone.
You touch my cheek then pull away.
I want to grab but see you strung and wrapped.
Frayed edges hold your surfaces intact.

Weekend at Slaughter Beach

The beach is strewn with shark heads,
left to rot by red-faced fishermen impatient when the tide cuts out.
Abandoned shells of horseshoe crabs and baby mussels
surface in the muck.

My friends' beach house, well-built and seasoned,
is carpeted in blues and greens that have faded in the sun,
the ancient, weathered frame giving shelter to the compromises,
baby talk, and care that make their marriage work.

Gin at noon, margaritas at three, "juice" at five,
and in between, my search for shells.
I run on wave-packed sand, then lie prone,
basting in the sun: a truce of rest
on decks that shimmer in the heat of early August afternoons.

Next morning, six am, a guest on edge, I'm up and frowning,
sweep the sea, spot a heron, poised, alert, and blue,
perched in mud and priesting shore as gentle waves
lap chorus to her early morning song.

The kids Hank helps:
raw energy left floundering in the sand.
Stripped of shells, they struggle to protect
their risks and fears of loving.
Steve, hung by his wrists in first grade
for rolling in the mud in pants his parents
insisted he keep white while playing on the shore.
John, the town whore's kid.
Drunk, she beat him up or left him for a week.
Sober, has him check in on the hour like clockwork tides,
his fingernails chewed to calloused knots.

I fear their traps, those stalwart citizens
who know no more of love or energy and strength
than what they find in JC Penny catalogs.
What's sold for love is polyester easy-care, high starch food,
and the latest joys that plastic makes convenient.
Anger boiling in the fat lashes out of bloodshot eyes
and cheeks with broken veins.

Trailers banked on piles, new laundry rooms,
and Swanson's Hungry Men sustain alike the ladies of the night
and wives of fishermen, starched smug in their opinions.
Fearful lives. The beaches rot with dreams.

After My Bike Crashed

Satyr-like, you prance naked in the moonlight under pines,
a sensualist of fact and awkward questions.
Stretched in the webbing of your rusty chair,
I hold my arm's sling tight to my chest,
my fingers stumble through the thick, dark curls
you cut too close. I tease you:
a Samson shorn, you'll lose your charm.
We talk about your work:
you're a 9-5 emperor with no clothes on.

Hungry, you undress me with your eyes, laughing in the shadows.
You pluck my breasts like ripe fruit
and guide my mouth to the firm berries
growing wild in the hillocks of your chest.
My lips tangle in matted grass,
the night air lush with smells of honeysuckle and damp earth.

I bury your head between my legs.
I want to hold you under till you beg for breath,
but the chair collapses with our weight.
Laughing, we grab air and plunge deeper than we'd been before.
You fall spent, throbbing, resting on my broken wing.

Your son drops by the next day after school
and startles me with eyes that watch unnervingly like yours.
For fifty cents, he offers help to pick the heavy clusters
of hot strawberries ripening in my yard.
Clumsy together, we bake biscuits, mash the fruit,
and stuff ourselves with shortcake,
smearing chins and fingers with the gaudy juice.
I bend to kiss his head and catch his special smell:
damp with concentration, my brother smelled the same each spring.

I imagine you.
I still taste your body, smearing sweet against my skin.
He likes to talk and watches me.
My dress is hot pink cotton and clings too tight,
stuck to my flanks.
My right arm in its harness binds my breast:
he asks me if you'd called,
not trusting to your memory, lost in The Golden Bowl.
He reaches out to touch the lump that holds my bones in place
and wonders if I'm scared to ride again.

I ache the next morning. My broken bones are mending.
Aspirin and coffee soothe my feathered knots of pain,
but I am scared. Your abandoned, playful sex stings old wounds:
longing to be rocked back to the utter calm of loving, I feel
the slender fingers of another stroke my cheek,
pressed tight against his chest,
friend and dear friend who shadowed my life,
sun to my moon, storm to my strife.

Instead, priestess of the kitchen, I conjure your arched brow,
hooked like the cusp of the new moon, tracing my right breast.
Next time, I'll bring you breakfast in bed,
white wine and strawberries steeped in crystal bowls
and served with my mother's silver.

A Man I Know

for Charlie Capek

A man I know with heart of am
once told me as a child
he'd lived a place with minds of seem
days of know and seasons mild.

Seasons mild were joys of spring
days of know were green.
But minds of seem, those men of RIGHT,
made beauty into mean.

All things were either neither nor,
a thesis, numbered, made.
All know was known, the seasons sure,
and green a spectrum shade.

But it seems in this solemn world
this world of know and future past,
there lived a boy of am and twelve
with laughs of know and grins of ask.

His days were sun. His pockets green
stuffed secrets string and rusty nails.
With grimy hands and grin of am
he built a world of words and feel.

A world of secrets green and ask
(a day of know was a subtle thing)
and the place of seem or neither passed
and the world was am and praise and spring.

Stepson

for Ed Capek

Saying goodbye at 86th and Lex,
you're full of yourself and awkward
with the energy and harness of your fifteen years,
tall now, almost up to me, your "grossefusse."
Your size tens are bigger than my own.
(But yours are supposed to be,
a man's you tease, and con me out of tokens
and our omelets from the Patio at Macy's).

Ole Ed, a gracious wit,
you take pride in keeping to yourself.
Why should you want to share much more
with parents drifting in and out of phase?
I never plan, you tell me, proud of ease.
No wonder, with the fine examples we've displayed,
your twice-pruned family tree.
I point that out. You grin and disagree:
examples of how not to (love) but never say the word.

This is the summer you turn sixteen
and learn to drive back home in Minnesota,
envy of all the kids out here.

Out of my life, never in for long,
yet I know the texture of your hair,
your flat foot's arch, your crooked grin:
so much my own, yet not.

That summer of 101 Dalmations,
you sat in my lap and snuggled, then slyly started whistling,
"Cruella de Ville, I think of you still…"
Cruella stepmother.

Other jokes, old riddles,
fragile ties that give us something tangible to share
when talk's not easy: What's new?
"New York, New Jersey, Newbraska!"
Remember Falling Rock, the lost, old Indian Chief
whose mother put up signs along the road to find him?
We'd shout up the steep hill along the road to the country Dairy Queen,
"Chief Falling Rock, where are you?"

Big Chief, I wonder when you're my age where you'll be
and what you'll think of me who loves you
but can't seem to share more than cheers for evading, once again,
the evil Darth Vader on a late spring afternoon
and (this you'd think was gushy)
crying as the train pulled out of Newark, heading south through rain.

Peacock in sneakers, you're proud and tough and slightly vain,
but shy and not yet sure of all the presence you'll command,
a sudden blessing, late sunlight streaking Jersey Meadows.
Family wastelands sparkle with the magic of unexpected daylight.

You'd conclude by telling me I wrote a sneaker poem with lots of sole.
Archly. Run fast, Nike.

Susie

Plunged again into loving
I worry about your cough
the wart on your thumb
your cigarettes and bad sinuses.

You shimmer in the early morning light and ruffle my feathers.
My heart's in my throat,
even a wheeze threatens.
I fear losing the sheer joy of you.
Panic. This is the way I imagined I'd feel
gazing at the crib of the baby never born:
a fierce protection for the fragileness,
the miraculous energy of such lifeforce.

It's the same helpless longing limned those summers
I sang Ed asleep on his narrow boy's bed,
For the moment cool and curled in his growing, aching legs.

Odd, this loving, the wonder at it all,
all my senses jangling, blurred with memories
of those who mattered most and shaped the part of me I trust the least.

You're a trip.
I've fooled you into loving me.

I Dream of Dead People

I dream of dead people.
They visit me mornings, early, before first light.

Seated at ceremonial tables, chatting with neighbors,
my Uncle Clint wears a smart tan leather jacket and plaid tie.
    He usually dressed in old overalls.
I pat his shoulder. He turns and hugs me.
Pleased to see me, but not especially surprised,
My Aunt Agnes smiles, waves, and continues her conversations.
She always was very chatty. As a child, I cherished her stories.

My cousin Marjorie, dead now for decades, reminds me this is
    a celebration,
a memorial for her father, John, the butcher, who never had a sendoff.
(I never knew why.)
I remember him tall, with strong hands, and kind eyes. His mother-in-
    law Mary was
my grandmother's older sister (all nine children came from Larne,
    in steerage,
in batches, in the 1880s. Made new lives in Brooklyn, Dallas, and
    New Jersey.)

Marjorie terrified me. She was stern, head of school, and
a close friend of my father's. But she brooked no favors for relatives.
I was always in trouble.
Our elementary school, Absalom Grundy, was eventually named in
    her honor.
I preferred Absalom Grundy, which always had a ring to it.

That night in my dream, Marjorie greeted fancy couples downstairs
    at her lovely home
where she'd lived all those years with her parents and drove
    new Chryslers.
An "old maid," she'd never married.
She spent summers on the Maine coast with a woman "friend."
And when her parents both died, she retired, then moved up there
    year-round
with one of her "friends."

In my dream, I tried to tell her that night with excitement that I was
    "one" like her.
But she never gave me the chance. Just ushered me upstairs to the dinner
where I greeted my beloved uncle and aunt. They were glad to see me.

On another night, my father-in-law came for a visit, at a conference in
    Wisconsin.
Wayne and I ate lunch at the counter, just the two of us,
while Sue, my wife, impressed the others with her wise words in small
    rooms.
Wayne and I sat on stools, eating tuna fish sandwiches, drinking
    lemonade,
making small talk. For thirty-three years, he never knew what to do
    with me.
He thought he'd failed Sue because she'd never married.
"Wayne," I'd say, "You never failed Sue! She found ME!

He didn't know what to do with that either. But he was wearing
a gorgeous jacket made of cream-colored, coarsely woven fabric, looking
    very handsome.
He usually wore old hunting pants and Pendleton wool shirts.
Sue and I were given a dragonfly token that allowed us
to park our camper while Wayne and I ate lunch,
while Sue conferenced, where later we slept.

On another night, when I couldn't sleep (or so I thought),

there was my beloved Ruth, a dear friend who'd died last April.

She lounged in a damask armchair, her arm draped insouciantly over
the chair's back.

I did a doubletake: "You're HERE!"

But I'm not asleep, I thought. How could you be here?

Not one to miss an opportunity, I asked her,

"Why did you die? How could you leave us all to mourn, to go on
without you?

Why did you have to die?"

Tears streamed down my sleeping face, which was wet when I woke up.

She gestured as she'd often done, palms up, arms extended, shrugging
her shoulders.

She looked me in the eyes and smiled. But did not apologize.

Pink

Last Tuesday, I thought about dying my hair pink.
But... What would people think?
Not acting your age, my dear?

And where's the rage in pink, after all?
I need some overt expression of rage, spelled R A G E.

Grey does speak volumes: wisdom, experience.
Or long and black, like Native friends my age.
Shiny or opaque, but BLACK. With shared style and a common language.

But still I think pink. Punk. Another rebellion at 81? Yes!
Pink, just pink, caressing the tips of my short gray hair.
But, but...

Even with the armor of punked pink hair,
I wouldn't know words to speak
to those I meet on the street
or nod to in grocery lines.
Or, even more awkward, others with hair dyed pink:
I'd be tongue-tied, a silly old lady not aging with grace:
Who does she think she is?

Too old for hip.
I do realize I no longer have the patience or rhythm
of a person who dyes her hair pink.
Not even words to meet the expressions that I'd meet.
Maybe lavender? Or blue? Blue.

My grandmother occasionally had blue in her bold white hair.
Where did that come from? Did I imagine that?

She always knew what to say though. And it wasn't punk.
Usually it was some version of "speak softer, dear."
Which I never did. Usually yelling (loudly)
"this is who I am, ME!" At least to myself.
Even when we played canasta.

Now I hesitate, curious: can I just imagine pink?
And act accordingly?

Asylum

The Maya of the Yucatan invented writing, calendars, and a
    number system
that counted in the millions. Made tools and pottery, sang songs,
built ball courts, pyramids and temples, created public plazas
with monumental columns that told their history. 3rd century AD.

The Aztec in the Valley of Mexico built warrior statues to guard
    their temples.
They too made calendars: one, like ours, the other sacred, with symbols
marking sounds or words. They left books with rich depictions of their
    daily lives,
their legends, their beliefs. 13th and 14th centuries.

The Inca in Peru built an empire, 16 million people. In 1400s AD.
They used knots and cords for numbers, intricate skill recording myths
    and history.
These khipus, "language of animals," strung textured cords
commanding 95 "syllables" of color, touch, and direction.
    Let that sink in:

Touch as well as sight. Makers, readers had to know the different feel of
    vicuna, alpaca,
others that lent their coats to different cords of meaning.
Syllabic systems like our own, marks that set our speech, count symbols
    in a similar range.
But the Inca used touch. Touch! 95 locks of color, touch,
    and direction.
I wake up thinking about this.

These are ancestors, Americans, people of Central and South America
whose descendants seek asylum at our borders. Instead of safety,
    we aim teargas,
separate children from parents, call them "alien," "criminal," these
    noble people
who had their histories stolen, seeking refuge from their countries' wars
    our people started.

Some seekers, blood mixed for centuries with their conquerors,
are likely people of the touch, who used intricate knots and textured cords
to share their daily lives and myths, people who understood
the language of animals. I ache to welcome them.

Three dimensions, starting at our fingertips.
I touch your cheek, imagining a different world.

ABOUT THE AUTHOR

Mary Ellen Capek has had varied work as a professor, university administrator, national nonprofit executive, philanthropy researcher, organizational consultant, and writer. She finished her Ph.D. in contemporary poetry from the University of Wisconsin, Madison in 1973, but over the years, poetry took a back seat to her research and other writing. This is her first collection of poems.

Besides this collection, Mary Ellen is also working on a quasi-memoir and collection of selected, previously published prose writing (and a few poems) trying to explain how she got from studying poetry and teaching writing to organizational consulting. Tentatively titled *The Power of Naming*, this hybrid volume will be published in 2025.

Mary Ellen's papers are archived at the Schlesinger Library, Radcliffe (National Council for Research on Women-related publications, speeches, and correspondence); the Rockefeller Archive Center (the Rockefeller Brother Fund research, locked for 20 years); Indiana University/Purdue University Indianapolis Library (women in philanthropy/diversity in philanthropy research, speeches, correspondence and notes); the University of Denver (women in higher education research and materials); and the Hilda Raz archives, University of Nebraska—Lincoln (poetry and miscellaneous correspondence).